I0817099

BY ANNIE BRIGHT

CONTENT CONSULTANT
John P. Rosa, PhD
Associate Professor
Department of History
University of Hawaii at Manoa

An Imprint of Abdo Publishing
abdobooks.com

abdobooks.com

Published by Abdo Publishing, a division of ABDO, PO Box 398166, Minneapolis, Minnesota 55439.

Printed in the United States of America, North Mankato, Minnesota.
052022
092022

Cover Photos: Mio Buono/Shutterstock Images, map and icons; Shutterstock Images, pineapples
Interior Photos: Eddy Galeotti/Shutterstock Images, 4–5; Red Line Editorial, 7 (Hawaii), 7 (North America); Ronen Zilberman/AP Images, 10–11, 43; Jeff Whyte/Shutterstock Images, 13; Shutterstock Images, 15 (flag), 15 (fish), 26, 34; Ian Fox/Shutterstock Images, 15 (bird); Tino Fotografie/Shutterstock Images, 15 (flower); Lorraine Logan/Shutterstock Images, 15 (seal); Library of Congress, 16; Shane Myers Photography/Shutterstock Images, 20–21, 31; Alexander Demyanenko/Shutterstock Images, 23, 45; MNStudio/Shutterstock Images, 28–29; Mia Shimabuku/Bloomberg/Getty Images, 36–37; Erik Nuenighoff/Shutterstock Images, 41

Editor: Marie Pearson
Series Designer: Joshua Olson

Library of Congress Control Number: 2021951411

Publisher's Cataloging-in-Publication Data

Names: Bright, Annie, author.
Title: Hawaii / by Annie Bright
Description: Minneapolis, Minnesota : Abdo Publishing, 2023 | Series: Core library of US states | Includes online resources and index.
Identifiers: ISBN 9781532197529 (lib. bdg.) | ISBN 9781098270285 (ebook)
Subjects: LCSH: U.S. states--Juvenile literature. | Western States (U.S.)--Juvenile literature. | Hawaii--History--Juvenile literature. | Physical geography--United States--Juvenile literature.
Classification: DDC 996.9--dc23

Population demographics broken down by race and ethnicity come from the 2019 census estimate. Population totals come from the 2020 census.

CONTENTS

CHAPTER ONE

THE ALOHA STATE

The blue-green water ripples gently past a group of snorkelers. The snorkelers float on the surface of the water with their heads down. The shallow water reveals coral growing on the bottom. A sea turtle swims by. Soon the snorkelers find themselves swimming among butterfly fish, yellow tangs, angelfish, triggerfish, and other beautiful sea life. People can even spot the state fish, the humuhumunukunukuāpuaʻa. Hanauma Bay on the Hawaiian island Oahu is putting on a show for its visitors.

Hanauma Bay attracts many snorkelers.

ALOHA

Hawaii's nickname is the Aloha State. Aloha is the most commonly used word in Hawaii. It can mean both hello and goodbye. It also means other things including love, generosity, and listening. It is a lifestyle in which people live with love. Hawaiians believe that each person is important to every other person. They call it the aloha spirit.

WHERE IS HAWAII?

The State of Hawaii is located in the Pacific Ocean 2,397 miles (3,858 km) west of San Francisco, California. Eight major islands make up the state. From west to east they are Niihau, Kauai, Oahu, Molokai, Lanai, Kahoolawe, Maui, and Hawaii. The state of Hawaii is named after the island of Hawaii, which is often called the Big Island. It is the largest of the islands. More than 100 other tiny islands and bits of land make up the Hawaiian Islands.

Honolulu is the largest city in Hawaii. It is also the state capital. Honolulu is located on the southeast side of the island of Oahu. Kailua on Oahu and Hilo on the

MAP OF HAWAII

Hawaii is a state made up of islands. How does this map help you understand how the ocean influences life in Hawaii?

PERSPECTIVES

HAWAIIAN LANGUAGE

The Hawaiian language has only 12 letters in its alphabet. These letters are the vowels *a*, *e*, *i*, *o*, and *u* and the consonants *h*, *k*, *l*, *m*, *n*, *p*, and *w*. In addition, two diacritical marks represent other sounds. An okina (ʻ) means there should be a brief pause between letters. The kahako is a line over the top of a vowel (ū). It means that the vowel sound should be lengthened. By the mid-1900s very few people spoke Hawaiian. A move to revive the language began in the 1980s. College professor Larry Kimura first started a radio program and then a school to help a new generation of Hawaiians learn their native language.

Big Island are other large cities. Kahului is the biggest city on Maui. Kapaa is Kauai's largest city. Other than Oahu and the Big Island, the islands are largely rural or populated with small towns and cities.

Hawaii claims many firsts. It was the first state made up of only islands. It was the first to have once had a monarchy and the first located in the tropics. There is a lot that makes Hawaii unique among the states.

STRAIGHT TO THE SOURCE

Novelist Mark Twain visited the Hawaiian Islands in 1866. The experience meant so much to Twain that he spoke about Hawaii in a speech many years later:

> *No alien land in all the world has any deep strong charm for me but that one, no other land could so longingly and so beseechingly haunt me, sleeping and waking, through half a lifetime, as that one has done. . . . Other things change, but it remains the same. For me its balmy airs are always blowing, its summer seas flashing in the sun; . . . in my nostrils still lives the breath of flowers that perished twenty years ago.*

Source: Mark Twain. *Mark Twain in Hawaii: Roughing It in the Sandwich Islands, Hawaii in the 1860s*. Mutual Publishing, 1990, p. xxxiii.

CONSIDER YOUR AUDIENCE

Adapt this passage for a different audience, such as your younger friends. Write a blog post conveying this same information for the new audience. How does your post differ from the original text and why?

Lanikū'uwa'a

HISTORY OF HAWAII

The first people came to Hawaii by canoe in approximately 400 CE. Historians believe they came from the Marquesas Islands in Polynesia. By the 900s more settlers came from Tahiti. All of these travelers crossed thousands of miles of ocean. They used the stars, birds, and currents to guide their boats. Early Hawaiians farmed the land and fished. They irrigated taro fields. Taro is a root vegetable. They built fish ponds and grew many types of sweet potatoes.

Some people still make voyaging canoes similar to the ones that brought the first people to Hawaii.

By the 1700s the peoples of the Hawaiian Islands had a complex society. Chiefs ruled communities. People believed the chiefs were descendants of the gods. The communities fought one another for territory on the islands.

PERSPECTIVES

THE TARO PLANT

People have grown the taro plant in the Hawaiian Islands since the first Polynesians brought it. Legends say the first Hawaiian came from the taro plant. Some scientists believe it is the world's oldest farmed crop. The taro plant is very important to the Native Hawaiian culture. When the root of the taro plant is cooked, peeled, mashed, and mixed with water, the mixture becomes poi. Poi is a staple of the Hawaiian diet. This pale purple paste is a healthy starch. Poi is traditionally eaten with fingers alone. Fresh poi is sweet. Poi left to sit for a few days is sour but still tasty.

EUROPEAN CONTACT

British captain James Cook was the first European to visit Hawaii. He and his crew landed on Kauai in 1778. He called the group of islands the Sandwich Islands in honor of the British Earl of Sandwich.

A statue of King Kamehameha I stands outside of the Hawaii Supreme Court building.

The next 100 years saw great changes in the Hawaiian Islands. European ships stopped to refill their water supplies. The Native Hawaiians traded for many kinds of goods, such as metal tools. Meanwhile, Native Hawaiians battled one another for control of the islands. King Kamehameha I defeated other rulers. He united the islands in 1810. He and his descendants ruled the islands for almost 85 years. King Kamehameha I died in 1819. His son was too young to rule alone. So the king's wife, Kaahumanu, ruled for him.

In 1820 Christian missionaries from the United States arrived. The missionaries worked to convert

Native Hawaiians to Christianity. They created a Hawaiian alphabet, taught reading, and recorded the islands' history. But they also tried to make the Native Hawaiians become more like white Americans.

Queen Kaahumanu supported the building of schools and encouraged Native Hawaiians to learn to read. She became a Christian and got rid of the kapu system, the set of cultural and spiritual laws. She replaced them with Christian laws, which

THE HAWAIIAN HULA DANCE

When people think of hula dancing, they may think of women wearing grass skirts. In fact the traditional hula dance is done by both men and women. They do not wear grass skirts. The hula is an ancient dance with religious roots. It was used in ceremonies and to honor and entertain the Hawaiian chiefs. The movements in the hula tell stories. People continue to practice the traditional hula today. The modern hula with grass skirts now entertains visitors from around the world.

HAWAII

QUICK FACTS

Hawaii's state symbols are important to the people of the state. Why do you think each of these symbols is special to people in Hawaii?

Abbreviation: HI
Nickname: The Aloha State
Motto: *Ua mau ke ea o ka 'āina i ka pono* (The life of the land is perpetuated in righteousness)
Date of statehood: August 21, 1959
Capital: Honolulu
Population: 1,455,271
Area: 10,932 square miles (28,314 sq km)

STATE SYMBOLS

State bird
Nēnē

State flower
Yellow hibiscus

State fish
humuhumu-nukunuku-āpua'a (reef triggerfish)

State mammal
Hawaiian monk seal

Queen Liliuokalani was the last monarch of Hawaii.

gave her more power. She also protected Hawaii from foreign invaders.

European diseases were also new to the Native Hawaiians. Many died. By the 1890s fewer than 40,000 Native Hawaiians were left.

ANNEXATION TO THE UNITED STATES

In the late 1800s, American sugar planters in Hawaii sold a lot of sugar to the United States. Then the United States raised the tax people had to pay to import sugar from other countries. Sugar planters worried they would make less money because of this fee. They wanted Hawaii to be annexed by the United States. Then they wouldn't have to pay the fee.

In 1893 the planters overthrew the Hawaiian queen Liliuokalani. They called on the United States to send forces to help. Native Hawaiians held large protests against US control of the islands. Some Americans, including President Grover Cleveland, thought it was wrong to overthrow the queen. But Cleveland left office in 1897. The next president was William McKinley. He saw the Hawaiian Islands as an important ship base for war. The islands became a US territory in 1898. Hawaiian kings and queens no longer ruled.

In 1919 a Hawaiian delegate asked the US Congress to consider Hawaii's statehood. The matter was considered over several decades. But it didn't have enough support. In 1941 Japanese forces attacked Pearl Harbor. This was a US naval base near Honolulu. This attack drew the United States into World War II (1939–1945).

After the war, statehood was again discussed. In 1959 Congress and the Hawaiian people both voted to make Hawaii a state. It became the fiftieth state on August 21, 1959.

Today the state government of Hawaii has three branches. These are the executive, legislative, and judicial branches. The governor represents the executive branch. The legislative branch writes bills for potential laws and votes on them. The judicial branch is the court system. Unlike other states, Hawaii has just two levels of government. These levels are state and county. A mayor and council lead each county government.

STRAIGHT TO THE SOURCE

Hawaiian territorial senator Alice Kamokila Campbell opposed statehood for Hawaii. Campbell testified before a US congressional committee in January 1946. She said:

> *I do not feel . . . we should forfeit the traditional rights and privileges of the natives of our islands for a mere thimbleful of votes in Congress, that we, the lovers of Hawaii from long association with it should sacrifice our birthright for the greed of alien desires to remain on our shores, that we should satisfy the thirst for power and control of some inflated industrialists who hide under the guise of friends of Hawaii, yet still keeping an eagle eye on the financial and political pressure button of [control] over the people in general of these islands.*

Source: John S. Whitehead. "The Anti-Statehood Movement and the Legacy of Alice Kamokila Campbell." *The Hawaiian Journal of History*, vol. 27, 1993, pp. 43–63. *CORE*, core.ac.uk. Accessed 26 May 2021.

WHAT'S THE BIG IDEA?

Read this excerpt and determine its main idea. Explain how the main idea is supported by details the speaker gives. Name two or three of those supporting details.

CHAPTER THREE

GEOGRAPHY AND CLIMATE

The volcanoes that make up the Hawaiian Islands are dormant except for Mauna Loa and Kilauea on the Big Island. Southeast of that island is the Kamaehuakanaloa Seamount. It is a growing underwater volcano that will break the ocean's surface in thousands of years.

Each island is different in many ways, but they share a volcanic background. Seawater, rain, and wind have eroded the older slopes. There are mountains, cliffs, deep valleys, and coastal plains. Crashing Pacific waves formed

Kilauea is an active volcano. This means it can still erupt.

HOT SPOT

Volcanic eruptions formed the Hawaiian Islands starting at least 70 million years ago. Hot magma from Earth's core shot upward. Eventually the erupting volcanoes built up land above the surface of the ocean. The place where the volcanoes began is called a hot spot. The earth's surface in the central Pacific moves very slowly to the northwest. The hot spot stays in the same place. As the earth's surface moved, the hot spot formed new volcanoes. The volcanoes popped up in a line. They formed a cluster of islands, which became the Hawaiian Islands.

many beaches. There are black, white, and red sand beaches. The color depends on the minerals that make up the sand. Much of the soil on the islands is fertile from the lava left behind by the volcanoes.

CLIMATE

Hawaii's climate is tropical and mild all year. There are only two seasons. These are summer, or dry, and winter, or wet. Summer lasts from May through October. Winter goes from November through April. Summer temperatures average 85 degrees Fahrenheit

Hawaii has many beautiful landscapes.

(29°C) at sea level. The average winter temperature at sea level is 78 degrees Fahrenheit (26°C). Higher elevations in the mountains are cooler.

Tropical moisture comes with the winds from the northeast. Mountains block the wind from moving to the southwest sides of the islands, causing greater rainfall in the northeast. The northeast side of an island might get as much as 400 inches (1,010 cm) of rain in a year. The southwest side might get only 9 inches (23 cm) in a year.

ANIMALS

Hawaii's isolated position in the Pacific Ocean means the islands have many endemic species of animals and plants. An endemic species is one that is found in only one place. The first species came to Hawaii millions of years ago. They traveled by water, by wind, or attached to birds. Later the settlers from Polynesia brought plants and animals. Europeans introduced more species when they arrived. Many of the new species wiped out the native plants and animals.

The tiny Hawaiian hoary bat is the only land mammal native to Hawaii. The Hawaiian monk seal lives in and along the water. It is the only other mammal native to Hawaii that spends time on land. Many of the other land mammals are escaped domestic animals that have turned feral. These include cats, dogs, cattle, goats, pigs, horses, and rabbits. Other introduced mammals include pronghorn antelope, mongooses, rats, and wallabies.

There are no native species of land reptiles or amphibians. There are native marine reptiles including sea turtles and sea snakes. Near the coastline live whales, dolphins, colorful fish, and other

PERSPECTIVES

ENDANGERED SPECIES

Hawaii has less than 0.2 percent of the land area in the United States. However, it has 44 percent of the nation's endangered species. This includes mammals, birds, reptiles, snails, insects, and plants. Many native species have no defenses against non-native species. The non-native species crowd out the native species. Some of the endangered species are the Hawaiian monk seal, Hawaiian hoary bat, nēnē, hawksbill sea turtle, and yellow hibiscus.

Hawaii's scarlet honeycreeper, or 'i'iwi, has a specially shaped bill that lets it drink nectar from tubular flowers.

sea species. Seabirds such as noddies and wedge-tailed shearwaters soar near the coasts. On land, forest birds include honeycreepers. In addition, approximately 10,000 native insect species live in Hawaii. As many as 90 percent of them live only in Hawaii.

PLANTS

Thousands of plant species thrive in the rain forests and gardens of Hawaii. Orchids and Hawaiian hibiscus are popular flowering plants. The 'ōhi'a is a flowering tree.

It is the most common tree native to the islands. Frangipani, or plumeria, blooms are called Hawaiian lei flowers because they are often used to make necklaces called leis. They are not native to the islands. There are 366 Hawaiian plant species listed as endangered or threatened. Some people are working to grow these plants so they do not disappear.

EXPLORE ONLINE

Chapter Three mentions the Kamaehuakanaloa Seamount. The website below gives some additional information about seamounts. What other facts can you learn about seamounts from this website?

WHAT IS A SEAMOUNT?

abdocorelibrary.com/hawaii

CHAPTER FOUR

RESOURCES AND ECONOMY

Hawaii has fewer natural resources than many other US states. For instance, it has no important mineral deposits. But the state has plenty of its own natural resources. Its natural beauty drives its economy.

The first hotel, a grass structure at the edge of the Halemaumau crater, was built in 1865. Today tourism is Hawaii's largest industry. Millions of visitors spend billions of dollars on the islands each year. Tourists come

Hawaii's beaches, including Waikiki Beach, draw many tourists.

from around the world. The tourism industry supports hundreds of thousands of jobs.

There is a lot for tourists to see and do. There are state and national parks, including Kokee State Park on Kauai and Hawaii Volcanoes National Park on the Big Island. On Oahu, museums and historical sites such as the Honolulu Museum of Art, the Bishop Museum, and the Iolani Palace are popular. A visitor can take a tour of all of the great Hawaiian beaches,

NORTH SHORE SURFING

Surfing is the most popular sport in Hawaii. It was developed on the islands. British lieutenant James King made the first written record of surfing in Hawaii in 1779. The North Shore area on Oahu is where big-wave surfing competitions began in the 1950s. From November through February, the waves can be more than 30 feet (9 m) tall. Professional surfing is big business there, with several surfing competitions during the winter months. Waimea Bay Beach Park is one of the best places to watch big waves.

Waimea Canyon is on the western side of Kauai.

such as Waikiki Beach on Oahu or the Punaluu Black Sand Beach on the Big Island. On Kauai, there are hikes through rain forests and through Waimea Canyon, which is often called the Grand Canyon of the Pacific. Snorkeling is another popular activity. Molokini Crater off Maui offers clear waters and a lot of marine animals to spot. If a tourist prefers to be less active, there are hundreds of restaurants and other attractions.

PERSPECTIVES

THE HAWAIIAN COWBOY

In 1793 King Kamehameha received five longhorn cattle. Mexican cowboys came to teach the locals how to work the cattle. The local Hawaiian cowboys became known as paniolos. Parker Ranch on the Big Island was once the largest privately owned ranch in the United States. The ranch continues to thrive today. Robert Kamuela "Sonny" Keakealani Jr. began working at Parker Ranch in the 1970s. He is a fourth-generation paniolo. He said of the road that runs in front of the ranch, "I remember a time when there were more cowboys on horses than cars driving along this road."

AGRICULTURE AND FISHING

Agriculture is also important to Hawaii. The state has fertile soil for growing crops. Sugarcane and pineapples were the most important crops since before statehood. Sugarcane plantations were huge. The planters brought in workers from China, Japan, and Portugal in the 1800s. Then people from the Philippines, Puerto Rico, and Korea came in the 1900s.

Today agriculture is a smaller part of the state's economy. But fruits, vegetables, nuts, flowers, and coffee are still grown in the islands' rich soil. Ranchers raise beef cattle.

Commercial fishing in the ocean is another important source of income. Tuna is one of the most commonly harvested fish. However, pollution and overfishing have caused fish populations to drop. Today Hawaii imports more than half of its seafood.

MANUFACTURING

Companies in Hawaii manufacture a variety of products. Some businesses refine oil for fuel. Manufacturers also produce cement, chemicals, and steel products. Rock, gravel, sand, and soil are readily available for use in construction and landscaping.

There are also clothing manufacturers. Most are located in Honolulu. These companies produce printed fabrics and clothing.

Living in Hawaii is expensive. But many people find the beauty and other advantages of the islands are worth it.

COST OF LIVING

There are struggles living in Hawaii. The cost of living there is higher than in other US states. The biggest reason for the high cost is that Hawaii is surrounded by water. Almost all consumer goods have to be shipped to the islands by water or air. Housing costs are high because it's a popular place to live and there isn't a lot of land area. Housing is less expensive in rural areas away from the big cities. But residents in rural areas still face high costs for many things, including groceries. In addition, there are relatively few jobs outside of the tourism industry. Jobs in the tourism industry don't pay very well. Many people move to other states for more opportunities after working in Hawaii for a few years.

Still, for many Hawaii residents, the benefits of living in Hawaii outweigh the challenges. Some residents find ways to keep costs down. They may shop in bulk or look for sales to save money. In return, they can enjoy the islands' gorgeous weather and landscapes.

FURTHER EVIDENCE

Chapter Four discusses tourism, including to Hawaii Volcanoes National Park. Identify one of the author's main points. What evidence does the author provide to support this point? The article at the website below also discusses Hawaii Volcanoes National Park. Find a quote on this website that supports the main point you identified. Does the quote support an existing piece of evidence in the chapter? Or does it offer a new piece of evidence?

HAWAII VOLCANOES NATIONAL PARK

abdocorelibrary.com/hawaii

SURF SCHOOL

CHAPTER FIVE

PEOPLE AND PLACES

Hawaii has more racial diversity than the total US population does. In 2019 Asian residents made up 37.6 percent of the population. Hawaii residents who were two or more races made up 24.2 percent. White people made up 21.7 percent. Hispanic and Latino people were 10.7 percent. Native Hawaiians and Pacific Islanders made up 10.1 percent of the population.

This mixture of different races and cultures gives Hawaii a rich culture of its own.

Farmers markets, which create jobs and support local food growers, are popular in Hawaii.

This mixture shows up in almost every aspect of life in Hawaii. Food comes in delicious combinations of dishes from different cultures. Saimin is a noodle soup that originated in Japan, Korea, China, and other Asian countries. Loco moco is a breakfast dish created in Hawaii using both Asian and Western ingredients. It is a bowl of rice topped with a hamburger patty, gravy, and a fried egg.

Spam is a food that came to Hawaii from the continental United States during World War II. It has remained very popular

PERSPECTIVES

QUEEN LILIUOKALANI

Liliuokalani became queen after her brother died in 1891. In 1893 the queen was forced to step down when Sanford Dole, a powerful American businessman, took control of Hawaii's government. Queen Liliuokalani was never able to regain her throne. In addition to being a queen, Liliuokalani was a gifted songwriter. She wrote more than 160 songs. The most famous one was "Aloha Oe (Farewell to Thee)." It was written before the queen was forced out but was later known as a song of sorrow for the loss of her country.

with Hawaii residents. The canned meat can be fried, eaten with eggs, or used as a topping for other dishes. One favorite dish among Hawaiians is Spam musubi, which is a type of rice ball using Spam. For dessert, people in Hawaii like shave ice, which came from Japan. The ice flakes flavored with fruit juice are a welcome treat in the tropical heat.

PLACES

Honolulu is the biggest city in Hawaii. Its population is 350,946. The next largest city is East Honolulu with more than 50,000 residents. Honolulu is a major hub for international business, tourism, and the military. Polynesian migrants first lived on the southeastern side of Oahu in the area that became Honolulu.

Pearl Harbor is near Honolulu. It is still an active naval base. There are several museums and memorials there to honor all who served in World War II. The USS *Arizona* ship sank during the attack in 1941. The ship still lies beneath the harbor waters.

A museum was built above the sunken ship to honor the 1,177 sailors who died on it.

WAIKIKI BEACH

Waikiki Beach is a popular beach. It's on the south side of Honolulu. Hotels and restaurants line the edge of the white, sandy beach. But it didn't always look like this. Waikiki Beach used to be a swampy wetland that ran up to a narrow line of sand. Waikiki has been slowly transformed into a tourist attraction. The transformation was not always smooth. In 1913 local resident G. H. Buttolph told a newspaper, "Last Sunday I went to the beach with some tourist friends . . . and found the water as thick as mud."

One of the most famous people from Hawaii is former US president Barack Obama. He was born in Honolulu on August 4, 1961. In 2008 he became the first Black man and the first person from Hawaii to be elected president. Singer Bruno Mars was also born and raised in Hawaii. Surfer Carissa Moore is from the state too.

Many people enjoy surfing in Hawaii.

Surfing is the king of sports in Hawaii, but other sports are popular too. Baseball was brought to the Hawaiian Islands in the 1850s. Football is popular, as are cycling and windsurfing.

Hawaii is a state with great contrasts, whether among the people or the landscapes. The landscapes go from stark lava fields to lush rain forests. There are sandy beaches and huge cliffs. All of these things make Hawaii a popular place to visit and a special place to live.

IMPORTANT DATES

400 CE
The first settlers come to the Hawaiian Islands from the Marquesas Islands.

1778
Captain James Cook arrives in Hawaii. He is the first European to see Hawaii.

1819
Queen Kaahumanu begins ruling for King Kamehameha's young son. During her reign, she encourages people to learn to read, becomes a Christian, and changes the laws of her nation.

1865
The first hotel is built at the edge of the Halemaumau crater.

1891
Queen Liliuokalani becomes the last monarch of the Hawaiian Islands. An uprising of American sugar planters overthrows her in 1893.

1898
The Hawaiian Islands become a US territory.

1941
Japanese forces attack Pearl Harbor. This prompts the United States to enter World War II.

1959
The Hawaiian Islands become the fiftieth state on August 21.

2008
Barack Obama becomes the first Black man and the first person from Hawaii to be elected president.

STOP AND THINK

Tell the Tale

Chapter One describes a snorkeling trip at Hanauma Bay. Imagine you are making a similar snorkeling trip at this bay or another one. Write a paragraph describing what you see around you as you snorkel.

Surprise Me

Chapter Three discusses the weather and climate in Hawaii. After reading this book, what two or three facts about weather and climate in Hawaii did you find most surprising? Write a few sentences about each fact. Why did you find each fact surprising?

Take a Stand

The cost of living in Hawaii is high. Some people think it is worth it. Others do not. What do you think? Would the benefits outweigh the high cost of living for you? Why or why not?

Another View

Chapter Two discusses how Hawaii became part of the United States. As you know, every source is different. Ask a librarian or another adult to help you find another source about this topic. Write a short essay comparing and contrasting the new source's point of view with that of this book's author. What is the point of view of each author? How are they similar and why? How are they different and why?

GLOSSARY

annexed
joined together, often with something larger

beseeching
anxiously begging for something

diacritical
a mark written by a letter to change its pronunciation

dormant
temporarily inactive

economy
a place's system of goods, services, money, and jobs

fertile
rich in nutrients for growing plants

hub
a center of activity

irrigate
to water crops through human-made means, such as pipes

magma
molten rock within the earth

missionary
a person who is working for a religious goal, usually to spread his or her faith

monarchy
a country that is ruled by a king or queen

ONLINE RESOURCES

To learn more about Hawaii, visit our free resource websites below.

Visit **abdocorelibrary.com** or scan this QR code for free Common Core resources for teachers and students, including vetted activities, multimedia, and booklinks, for deeper subject comprehension.

Visit **abdobooklinks.com** or scan this QR code for free additional online weblinks for further learning. These links are routinely monitored and updated to provide the most current information available.

LEARN MORE

Loomis, Jim. *Fascinating Facts about Hawaii.* Watermark Publishing, 2019.

Messner, Kate. *Pearl Harbor.* Random House, 2020.

INDEX

About the Author

Annie Bright lives in Missouri and writes children's books. She enjoys traveling and visiting beautiful places around the country.